USA

A

is for

African American

These are our Black friends in America who descended from ancestors in Africa.

B

is for

bindi

This is the small red dot worn on the forehead by some married women in India and Southeast Asian countries.
The dot can be a sign of their culture and religious beliefs.

C

is for
Christian

These friends believe that God sent his son, Jesus to show us how to love one another.

D is for diversity

The way we look, what we believe, and the things that we like to do, make each person special and make the world an interesting and beautiful place.

E

is for
Earth

This is the home for all of the people and animals in the world.

F

is for

flamenco

This is a
lively form of
music and dance
celebrated in
Southern Spain.

G

is for

grow

The more we grow in our understanding of other people, the more we can practice love.

H

is for

Hispanic

These are our
Spanish speaking
friends of
Latin American
or Spanish descent.

I

is for
immigrant

These are our brave
friends moving to a
new country in the hope
of a better life.

J

is for
Jewish

Our Jewish friends
believe in God
and the Torah,
which are the laws
that were given
by God for how to live life.

K

is for

kimono

This is a traditional
Japanese dress which
represents Japanese
culture and heritage.

L

is for
love

This is a special feeling you have in your heart that makes you cherish your family and friends. Love always wins.

M

is for

Muslim

These are our friends
who practice Islam
and believe in God and
the prophet, Muhammad.
They study the teachings
of the Koran.

N

is for
Native American

These friends are the indigenous people from North America who have always had a deep respect for the land and believe in living in harmony with nature.

O

is for
old

We look up to and
respect older people
because they are
wise and knowing.

P

is for

Pacific Islanders

These are our friends that are native to the 25 nations on more than 25,000 islands in the Pacific Ocean.

Q

is for

qipao

This is a Chinese dress that is worn for holidays and special occasions, like weddings. A Wedding qipao is usually bright red.

R

is for
respect

We show respect
by being kind
and polite
to others,
even if they are
different from us.

S

is for
Scandinavia

These are our friends
in the most northern
regions of Europe,
where it is cold and dark
in the winter.

T

is for

turban

This is a long cloth that is fashioned into a head wrap. Men and some women wear turbans to represent their religion and cultural beliefs.

U

is for

unique

Unique is a word that means each and every one of us is special.

V is for **variety**

Variety includes things that are different that make life fun and interesting.

W

is for
wheelchair

This is a special chair designed to help our friends who may be sick or have trouble getting around.

X

is for

Xenia

This is the Ancient Greek rule for showing hospitality and generosity to strangers and people from foreign lands.

y

is for
Yupik

**These are
our Alaskan and
Siberian friends
who thrive
in ice and snow.**

Z

is for
Zulu

These friends are part of the largest ethnic group in South Africa. Zulu bead jewelry is beautiful and tells the story of Zulu culture.

From Z to A and A to Z,
We celebrate diversity!
We all have things that make us unique,
Maybe how we look, think, or speak.

The world would be boring, dull, and plain,
If everyone looked and talked the same.
Embrace things that are different. Learn something new.
The world needs kindness from a kid just like you.

It's important to remember to see good in all.
You can do this even though you are small.
In our world, it's important to see
That everyone is as special as can be.

Library of Congress-in-Publication Data
available upon request.
Printed in the USA.
Book design by Davor Ratkovic

Made in the USA
Middletown, DE
03 December 2020